Youth Relics

Youth Relics

S. A. Musson

To order additional copies of this book, contact:
Xlibris Corporation
0800-891-366
www.xlibris.co.nz
Orders@Xlibris.co.nz
700243

Contents

IV

V

I

Desaturated

I.

You said it in muffled, rainy blues, and altogether too many words.
"I love you", you said.

Not to confuse—
With the pinks and pretences of candy-store confessions.
The type that can be measured in sideways glances;
defined, without words, for fear of
saying the *wrong* thing . . .
and reimbursed at the end of each week—if you skipped enough beats
to warrant a single, clipped "Hello."
(just trying to keep it cool, cool . . .)

Not . . .
like that.

And not like sunshine either.

II.

I know a man whose smile is like sunshine.
He speaks in honeyed tones;
that liquid gold I swear could thaw a thousand hearts.
I gave him mine, and he

ate it.

I gave him mine, and
tangled in a web of—
fragile whims
and
white-ivory
limbs,

I lost many things.

. . .If you met him, would you smile too? Or would you
turn grave and green like a jealous lover?

III.

If I had to choose another,
I would choose between bittersweet chocolate
and caffeine.

Affection in a pair of fawn-eyes
peeking through the hot steam feelers
of a cup labelled
'Mine',
and the intermittent cravings I have
for those cocoa-coloured,
tiny lies.

(more than that though,
I know you don't like either of them).

IV.

Each night,
I soak my skin in all these
kaleidoscope-dreams.
At dawn, I try to rinse them away, but . . .
into my pores they creep.
Into my sinews and bones they seep
until I am them,
and they are me.

V.

I. am. them.
And they are me.

VI.

You said it in muffled, rainy blues.
"I love you", you said.

But all these vivid intonations mean
Nothing
to you.

You don't see me in rose-red *or* blue.
You just ask that I fill you

With a blank lover's hues.

La la la-la

Yesterday
when all the stars fell out of the sky
I think they settled somewhere
between
your skin and
your bones and
I'll go straight to 'angel' before

"Umm,
nice to meet you . . ."

See, I've already dissected your parts
laid your ribs out side-by-side
and oh
they sparkle,
my friend.
They lie in perfect, fine lines like
pure,
pristine,
(you are)

profound.

Today all the lights in the sky have
gone out,
though.
And I know your hands shake when you're
alone at night.

"How are you . . .?"

You're similar to that feeling
of losing your breath and waiting for someone
else to catch it.
You're sorta
drowning in such a
tidy way.

From here there are
christmas lights
twinkling
in your hair.
I can
see
you
and I—
tomorrow, I

(should probably say hi, but . . .)

I'll spell beautiful with your insides.

Dead Girl

i don't know who you're trying to be, *alabastrine;* a ghost amongst the white noise of summer suburbia. listless and wandering, you leave your translucent fingerprints on the glass of all the warmer places, but steamy windows and the humble hearth hold no home for you.

why not, drop your anchor in my teacup? i've no home, hearth or even heart for you to call your own, but at least i can damn well see you; look you in those pretty eyes and keep you warm for a spell. if you'll let me, i'll descend inside you like weak tea and whisper, just barely, in the lukewarmest of tones:

you are not alone.

Falling Leaves

I want to
slide my fingers inside
your
ribcage.

(You talk like
falling leaves, and I)
have to know
what lies . . .

in all those
hard-to-reach places
where the
dust gathers.

From insects caught
in the
web of your
lifeblood
to the dark and dreary
corner
of
your
eye.

Only once I
am well acquainted
with the grit in your fingernails
and the
secrets you were saving for later—
Can I hold
your trembling fists
together
and truly appreciate
the way your
face
lights up like

wildfire in the
twilight.

The Star

My stomach opened wide, and a night sky was born from it.
Hope scattered like yellow confetti, a yellow glitter explosion, gentle yet, as
I wished upon each autogenic, self-indulgent star for something better.

and here you are.

Rainbow Ride

I keep one eye to the outside
of your kaleidoscopic mind.
Only fractured light, where once
I tumbled in torrents of colour
and vibrant dreams.
Soon, I will descend again
through red, green, blue
as a tiny prism:
Casting once more,
my splintered spectrum
next to yours.

Ain't No Easy Way Out

He tells me all about the things that hide
in his body, like I couldn't already hear
the tremors of tectonic teeth grinding
down on life's indigestibles
or the planet-pulse inside his chest:
murmurs about—how he'd crumple
worlds, just to know
himself and why
we all keep
spinning
'round
but

I don't have the answers.

So he looks up at me, laughs;
chokes on his drink
and I bite down

hard.

Migraine Weather

The sun's a spinning toy to this one,
laughs like a thunderclap when I'm a storm
inside a sigh and maybe if I were taller,
it wouldn't make my ears pop, electric
shock-stopped like hey—it's something half interesting
to kill time with before the next orbit.

But I'm a late sleeper, really, it's almost noon
I burn easy; hate the pressure, lose my appetite
whilst I'm praying for silent sundown
and the choppy weather's rarely ever
more than moaning while I wait
for it to pass.

II

Lungs

. . .

. . .Inhale.
To the thief and the vampire:
I am your Mother.
I taught you to live and breathe
in colours other than
cig-smoke, apathetic gray.

. . .

. . .Inhale.
To the prick and the coward:
You are nothing.
but a parasite, born, bled,
and nourished
on the very worst of me.

Ophelius

You're sinking into putrid and pretentious water brother, and it's not giving you back. Sinking till your teeth and your bones erode, till your every waterway is flooded; flooded, dams broken, overflowing, *choking*.

And now your heart is skipping beats much like it does when it thinks your lungs have become wings but they haven't, brother, they haven't, they are but urns, vessels, inseminated with your liquid notions, pleura full and bursting—blooming into aconite delusions of blues and whites.

Blues and whites, white, blue, now that's a colour, a colour better suited to your skin; she told you, she told you so, and you believed. And you're choking now brother, I know you are, stuttering, spluttering, all your insides on the outside; your throat heaving a cacophony of your mismatched ribs and your failing pulse. I heart it beat, beat, beat . . . beat and then I didn't.

How pretty you are, brother. You are drownéd, tangled and suspended in vine and flora, *liar, liar, liar, liar,* lost yourself I know, I know you did. You are Snow White hurling up her poison apple, or maybe just the core, the rotten, ripened core maybe, maybe you are feel-sorry-for-the-wounded-soldier brother you are, you are Ophelia never-quite-thought-hard-enough . . . you are . . . you are . . .

and we are not.

Catatonic

There is a place here. It is the colour of stretching your skin across torchlight and watching your veins crawl on the ceiling. It is the colour of closing your eyes and staring through the lids at artificial lights—you wish, you wish, you wish—they were real. It is not a place for living; for you alone have forgotten how. As in the womb, you drift unawares in a sheltered and gestational lack—

of everything.

You are the only one here. The only things truly alive are your thoughts . . . and my god, they are alive.

Deluded Agnostic

Please, please, find a way to leave.
You'd have destroyed me had me and my dreams here,
not bin' made of sterner stuff, you're outta control
firing blanks at all the wrong walls.
Not nearly enough to bring me down, but let me tell you, son,
I'm more than thoroughly unimpressed.
I'm cannon-fodder, while you're out here warring
with yourself, fighting drink with drug with twisted love
in the name of, well, me.

The calendar girl of your dream's barracks
where you lie rank and delirious, touching
yourself to this angel untouched, Mary, Mary
quite contrite; oh Magdalene, holy whore,
your contradiction, your drowned fantasy;
Lie, and fuck yourself for my virginity.

Estranged, lonely soldier, I was never an angel.
You make like all this worship might somehow
slay the opposition in your head, someday
You'll come home to me with the corpse,
his head on a stake, vanquished; you—validated,
The champion of your demons, and together
we'll march onward to that Promised Place
you don't believe in.

But I don't even remember what you look like.

So soldier on, sir.
Solider on.

Like Stars

everything's broken
but stars can still hold themselves
together, can't they?

Sinning Was The Easy Part

The catch snapped and I've released my blights unto the world,
Pandora told me not to look, but I'm so desperately seeking me,
I cannot stand to stay inside, to hide what I've possessed—
Too many lives and times and crimes and deaths,
the rotting in my chest, I guess
it's imminent at best.

You Were

A brief, waking dream
from the stuff of nightmares and
hallucinogens.

That Thing I Never Told You

witless twit
you won't admit
in blood or spit
the mud, the grit,
in life—admit
my heart won't fit
that tight-lipped slit
that soul, unlit
i won't submit
i can't permit
my love befit
you, lifeless git.

Realism

I'll make my wishes
when I find a single star
not already dead.

III.

Star Charting

I think the constellations in your eyes
are prettier than evening skies
But I still don't know—
what stars are like up close.

I spent endless nights on my porch
mapping your horoscope;
drowning in your tiny lights
until my lashes were soaked
in glitterdust.

I plucked them like flowers
from the sky.
Brought them inside and I
strung them up to catch my dreams.
Watched my walls aglow with
traces of you.

But, they didn't shine the same
as they'd been shining in the sky.
They didn't shine as bright, in fact,
they just burned my eyes.

Didn't help me sleep at night,
no twinkling lullaby . . .
Much the same as flowers do,
they simply shrivelled,

and they died.

Incandescent

i. like stardust; you remain visible long after your last living breath. constant. never ending but never more than twinkling lights from light years away. imploded way before i spat your name to the heavens on a lonely night nearly a year ago—fell asleep before the afterglow. but even from way out here, i've got nothing better to do than stare at something dead. prettiest thing i've seen this side of the sun. prettiest goddamn thing i've seen at all.

ii. i am the starlight strung between your fingers just as you are, mine, soft as angel's hair and twice as bright. threading gentle a labyrinth between us, a mesh of silver hopes to draw us closer, ah, little firefly . . . when our lucent fingers finally meet, those faint and starving in the dead of night will have something to shine about.

The Butter Knife Won't Cut It

Let us explore the art of speaking without speaking.
Let us meet and greet in the airspace
reserved for electromagnetic impulses,
body heat, and static cling.

Armies of fine hair at attention, our soldiers
huddle hushed and invisible
waiting for the calculated moment
to unleash their silent warfare upon us.

Scorn the flash grenade, superior artillery's at work
to keep us blind and debilitated:
We destroy each other, perfectly,
in a deathless siege of our own wants
unspoken.

Riddle of the Scales

I'm telling you now
I'll come away from this with the short end of the straw.
I'm the question; your dislocated indecision
Has me gobsmacked and hurling back and forth
like the pendulum or the grandfather clock—ticking away the time
but twice as violent—and no doubt
It's been a while now, I mean, I've been counting.

I don't have those dreams anymore
and if I do, rarely, you're in 'em, little lights
big eyes and all; that crackling quietude made for just my ears.
You instead of faceless whispers haunting
me, deliciously, now and again and heaven knows
I'm not complaining, I had sleeping with ghosts down to a fine art
however many years ago, I forget; I've got another reason
for all the X's on my calendar.

You, you and your topsy-turvy curvy act
trying to reach some silent harmony that's
One more hesitation away, one more switch-flip,
On and off, off and on, and off and
ultimately it results in nothing at all.
But if nothing at all feels this good,
then heaven knows
I want nothing more.

Enlightenment

i've run out of ways to describe
things that shine the way you do.
stars, fairy lights, angel dust;
ashes to all, all
all i've left to say is *you.*
maybe that's all
i should ever have said,
from the start.
you, you, you, you.
you, you, you.

Astrology Lesson

Librans are great till
you become the decision
they never quite make.

I've learned that 'wonderful'
is the correct way to spell,
excruciating.

I've learned patience
and a whole lot of love.

Consumerà

We exchanged stares like wildfire *(you started it)*. You boiled in my blood like a drug. You, you, you . . .
Set fire to my veins. Set fire to my—
brain.
Raced from the back of my eyes to the base of my spine and back to my fingertips so cold, cold to the touch; but now they
incinerate.
everything around me.
Try to sleep, but the sparks on my lashes light my walls with shapes that look and sound like you.
In the dark, I could touch them.
(in the dark I could touch you).
Sometimes, if I blink too fast or close my eyes, two of them will catch, and I go
up in flames.
all over again; hot, salty streams charring my cheeks—running relays to the corners of my mouth to pool in all the places I could have said something more than 'i *want* you.' But that's

all.

I.

do.

Inane

So long as the moon finds its home in the sky,
I'm enslaved to the one with lunatic eyes.
Waxing to waning to waxing again,
More of myself in those eyes
than my veins.

Mad Girl

Take the damn apple
No one ever called me Eve,
Just, 'crazy for you.'

An Insubstantial Thing

He is the one with matchstick fingertips.
The one with teethmarks on his tongue.
I would that he would strike,
once, twice, thrice.
Against by back; catch my
murder in the act
so we might descend
to Pandemonium: solid as smoke,
And mourn the passing of our tenderness.
I could hold him within,
had charcoal not chalked his name
in my lungs, with only ashes
to breathe.

Had he not burned to
little cinders—
our Hellfire dreams.

Theia Mania

Frenzied one, I was never your muse
still, you burn up with nervous fever
and down, down—you drag us both deeper.
Lunatic rush in the brain and the blood
into the sinews, my veins are a-flood
with second-hand phrases, shiny bright eyes
moon-shy exchanges, and
tiny white lies.

(I don't think I should kiss you, darling,
lest this fever further spread . . .)

(I think that if I kissed you, darling,
I'd kiss you fairly dead.)

I'll consecrate you in madness divine
I'll love you until you're sick in the mind
My tenderest onslaught, o' chemical war
my heart's not got eyes for you, love
it's got jaws.

(Don't think that I should love you, darling,
with this blight upon my breath . . .)

(I think that if I loved you, darling,
I'd love you quite to death.)

Wide Shut

everyone has eyes
for me but I can't decide
where to put them all.

All's Fair

There were no arrows—just an empty cannon.
Eros himself, the wretched lout
clambered well inside,
went up in smoke
and left
of me

the high velocity impact spatter.

IV

Postmortem Confessions

There's nothing left of me now, nothing but myself and all my human parts. I have bones, I have organs, I have skin and scars. I have a heart that's grown much too big for me and I don't care for it—too tired to keep the damn thing beating. Do you want it? Keep it. I'm giving it to you. Drop it or toss it away or let it grow dusty and dark on the shelf while you hold on to another's. Anything. I don't want it anymore and I know it'd be much happier in your hands for three seconds than beating away in this too-tight ribcage for the rest of a lifetime. Can't you just . . .?

'Cause I've fallen down as humans do and I'm in disarray. And I don't need another person here to hold me together—you know—I can do that on my own. I've done it many times before. I've rebuilt my skeleton from the ground up and I can take a farther fall and find it in me to stand up again. I know how to make all my dreams come true . . . But I don't want to, 'cause last night I dreamed I asked you to take me away, and you did.

Can't you just . . .?

I don't want to be strong anymore. I don't want to be upright, to be right, wise, self-sufficient or insightful. I don't want to be fascinating nor admirable. Tell me something I don't know. Tell me I am brainless and wrong. Pitiful. Lonely, helpless and broken. Are you listening? I give up. I give up. I am shattered and human and I want you to gather the pieces up in your arms and tell me it's alright; not because I need it, but because you make me smile. You make this overgrown and infantile heart skip beats and forget itself. You make it better.

You make it better and I don't want a better reason to want you.

Rayleigh Scattering

Did you know:
The thing that gives the sky its hue,
Is the same thing that makes
Your eyes so blue?

And you wonder,
Why I think so much of you.

The Divide Just Isn't That Great

he paints each side of a horizon,
but bluer still is the reason
i could never choose

                       between sky-high

and dispirited—i look

twice inside the same pair of eyes,
and swim only in my own
after all.

Between

Sometimes,
I feel like I could reach out and touch
all this

You   [distance.]   And I

might try
one day.

but I already know
what 'nothing' feels like.

Splitting the Atom

When you ask why my smile
is a spark that will not catch
My joy, a breath I choose to hold
I will keep my lips mostly pursed
and tell you there is no other reason
than my want not to destroy you
in a holocaust of love.

Better Yet

I forged my ribs from steel
not to vault their contents
(hidden from rough hands,
intruders—the whole world.)
but to keep you

far away
from me and that thing
clawing out at you

within.

23/12/11

Earth tells me that she's sorry
for the heart I'm left without
when she wrenched my ribcage open
and you
        came tumbling
                out.

Amantissima (Some People call it Falling)

Truth be told I'll always hold
more dreams than I've got snatchers.
My all kinds of everywhere:
trembling night-time breath songs,
for muted daytime sighs,
I hold myself at harm's length

and shatter
                    every time.

How She Is

I trade your rough hands
for ink and give my fondness
to an empty page.

V

The Games We Used To Play

Your kiss left poison whispers on my tongue.
Bitter implications for my lips alone—
I'm an addict for the subtext
while you're out there, lusting
for a liar.

I can't erase the feeling of your breath;
Rasping, from an icy mouth—but so
hot against my cheek when you told me
it wasn't enough.

I wasn't enough for you,

Liar.

Kick in the Shins

There's no sentimental value
to the blood at my feet
and no beauty, in the snow
in which I'm drowning
ankle-deep.
If by chance you could see me
without those frosted lashes
to frame;
then believe me, my love,
I would be as ugly
as you are vain.

Nameless Days

I could have sworn you were
Six feet taller
Just a year ago.
And I would've bet my life
that I caught a glimpse
of a more sinister shade of blue
in your eyes.

Back then, I would have died to know
what thoughts plagued the atmosphere
On cloudy days,
Or what happened when they tumbled
almost six feet under . . .

Of all the things that are lost
Scattered like glitter to the wind
I still remember clearly
just how tall you really were
when you unravelled at my feet.

Ghost of You

Echo . . .
                    Distance never
Meant a thing.
The
                    Ghost of you
Goes on
                    and
                              on.
Seep into the memory
That made you mine.

Michiyuki

I remember you,
I remember you
Sinking through, icy blue.

Tip-toed, barefoot and trembling to an underwater tune,
(To be submerged beneath the water is
to be submerged in you.)
I shivered, skipped, tripped and stumbled;
sought the virtue in your vice
but saw only my reflection, river-dancing on the ice.

Madman's Epitaph

my heart belongs to the sea
she drinks my dreams up for me
whispering waves; my secret in sand,
the veins of a river
as the lines of my hand.
and each grain of sand, a glint in the sky
breathe into being—
the dreaming
of ten thousand lives.

my heart belongs to the sea
drink watery dreams up for me
silent my lover; no
silent my wife
i belong to the sea,
so silence
my life.

The Curséd One

Once upon a time,
I could look up at the sky,
And I could fall asleep,
To the sound of lullaby,
Once upon a time,
I still wanted to know 'why'
And once upon a time—
When I felt sorrow
I would cry.

Tumble into Grace

Once, I had a knight with no armour.
he breathed pixie dust, feigning freedom
and they called him by a stranger's name
until I caved in beside him;
learned the lay of his brittle bones.

But he was born for brighter things

In exchange for being good and kind
they gave him faerie wings
and he rose, higher than happiness
spun-stuck no more in the lifeweb
of human suffering.

I swore I'd never put my head down
for love, but now even trees bow.
Their new ruler, a gypsy man; half man
whole now where his scars used to be
He bleeds the colour of the night sky.

I travel with him, the faerie king
he takes my hand and the rings I wore
on all the wrong fingers.
Once like the moon, always hiding
he learns now to lead me.

Together, we are learning
to tell raindrops from dewdrops
from faerie diamonds
in the wet earth-birth of rain.
each day, we see them afresh
with brand new lights
in our eyes.

Mirror Dream

You asked to see yourself in me
so I gave you a mirror and shed—pretences.
Lying still to let you in, your smell, like honey
sticks sweeter to my skin than sweat;
burns me up so I might beg
the kinda burn that begs a scar.

Breath fogs up the glass—the pulsing in my
hallowed water's getting wetter, even better:
I am the earth moans under you, soft
inhaling all your details, birthing summer in my core,
while you breathe hard as if for both of us
and gasp like god for air.

Le Quartier

I will live five million lives
and we will meet five million times
every time they clean the slate
I'll find you, love
again,
      again.

I will walk a million lands
and count a million grains of sand
my love will never go to waste
With you, adieu
to time
      to space.

I Talk to the Rain

Sunlight skims on milky skin
Trying to hold on, your wrists, those slim
slip-knot slips caught only in the wind
I say you belong to the weather, but you
wrought over like the weeping willow—
wisps of silk hair, whimper but softly
that all the world is steeped in silence.

Every season, a winter without water
Hearts well up to wither and I'm the only one
who still bothers to talk to the rain.
I pool in all your hollows, let my fingers roam
the ripple of your ribs and wonder,
to what I'd have to whisper
if the winter never came.